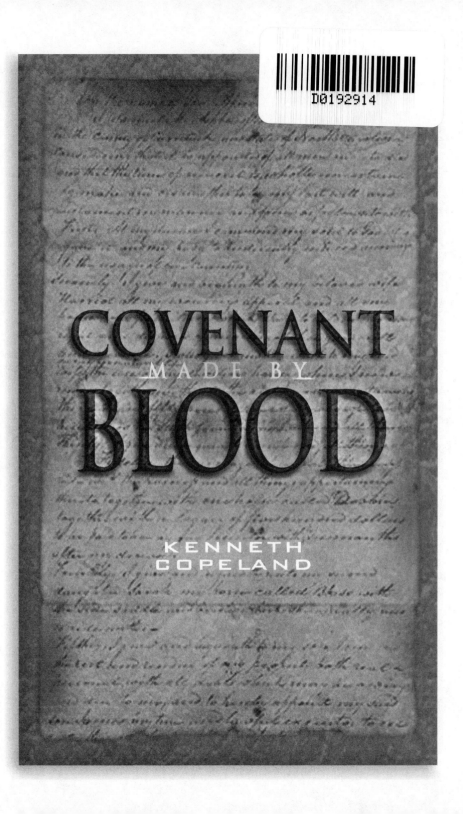

COVENANT
MADE BY
BLOOD

KENNETH COPELAND

COVENANT MADE BY BLOOD

KENNETH COPELAND

KENNETH
COPELAND
PUBLICATIONS

Covenant Made by Blood

ISBN 1-57562-697-7   30-0727

09 08 07 06 05 04   9 8 7 6 5 4

© 1989 International Church of the Word of Faith, Incorporated, now known as Eagle Mountain International Church, Incorporated, aka Kenneth Copeland Ministries

Kenneth Copeland Publications
Fort Worth, Texas 76192-0001

For more information about Kenneth Copeland Ministries, call 1-800-600-7395 or visit www.kcm.org.

Getting Started

You are about to uncover one of the most valuable discoveries that you could ever dig out of God's Word—the reality of your covenant with God. This revelation will touch every aspect of your life. It will help you receive your healing when you are sick. It will give you confidence that God will meet your financial needs. It will strengthen your marriage and family relationships. And, it will bring peace to your mind and joy to your soul.

In our modern Western civilization, we don't understand the blood covenant. However, without a revelation of the covenant, it is nearly impossible to grasp the strength and integrity of God's promises to us. Because of His covenant with us, God will keep His Word regardless of what it may cost Him. In our Western culture, this depth of commitment is a mystery. We have become too "civilized." Unfortunately, the more civilized a man becomes, the further he drifts from his commitment to keep his word. Today, it is not uncommon for people to lie, backstab and cheat.

> *Without a revelation of the covenant, it is nearly impossible to grasp the strength and integrity of God's promises to us.*

Why has integrity been lost? The answer lies in a lack of understanding the strength of covenant agreements. A blood covenant demands absolute, unwavering loyalty. Rediscovering the meaning of covenant relationship will turn the tide of Western man's lack of integrity to keep his word.

To seize the real meaning of the word *covenant,* you need more than just a definition. You need a revelation from Almighty God. The definition will only tell you what a covenant is. A revelation of *your* covenant with God will cause you to stand steadfast against the devil when he comes to destroy you. The mere definition does not have the power to uphold you against the storms of life.

Webster's Ninth New Collegiate Dictionary defines the word *covenant* as "a usually formal, solemn, and binding agreement: COMPACT, a written agreement or promise usually under seal between two or more parties especially for the performance of some action." These definitions could very well describe our modern use of the term *contract*.

> *God's covenant is to a thousand generations!*

Contracts are very familiar to us. However, we usually think nothing of trying to get released from the responsibility of them. Probably the best example of our general lack of loyalty is in marriage. More than half of the marriages entered into in America during the mid-1980's ended in divorce. In certain European countries, the rate is even higher. A marriage contract is two people promising to love and cherish one another "until death do us part," but in our society, it has become extremely easy to break that promise when the going gets rough.

The true covenant relationship is not easy to break. The strength of a covenant commitment is truly "until death do us part," and even then, the commitment is not over. Some man-made covenants were made to last up to eight generations. *God's* covenant is to a thousand generations!

Just consider: What would happen to the divorce rate if we responded to a failing marriage in the same way God responded to the fall of man? When man sinned and separated himself from God, God didn't replace him, He redeemed him. God was committed. That commitment eventually restored the relationship between man and God through the plan of redemption. Becoming covenant-minded will raise the level of our commitment to God's level and erase the word divorce from our vocabulary. When we will keep our commitment, even if it means our own hurt, we totally close the door to the devil. We will be committed to restoring broken relationships and refuse to allow Satan to steal, kill, and destroy our precious families.

The devil was powerless to ultimately destroy God's relationship with man because God's integrity left no room for evil to enter in and bring corruption. The devil will be powerless to destroy us when our integrity matches God's integrity. And a revelation of the strength of a covenant relationship is the only thing that can lift us to the level of God's integrity and commitment. That's what we're going to discover in the following messages and study guide.

"Wherefore take unto you the whole armour of God, that ye may be able to withstand in the evil day, and having done all, to stand."

Ephesians 6:13

God's covenant with you is eternally

sealed in Jesus' sacrifice.

TAPE/CD ONE
Covenant Practices

Through Our
Blood Covenant With
God, We Are His Family—
Receiving All His Authority,
Protection and Strength

The Union

FOCUS: "Wherefore take unto you the whole armour of God, that ye may be able to withstand in the evil day, and having done all, to stand. Stand therefore, having your loins girt about with truth, and having on the breastplate of righteousness; And your feet shod with the preparation of the gospel of peace; Above all, taking the shield of faith, wherewith ye shall be able to quench all the fiery darts of the wicked. And take the helmet of salvation, and the sword of the Spirit, which is the word of God" (Ephesians 6:13-17).

The Bible is a book of covenants; therefore, covenant terminology is threaded all the way through it from Genesis to Revelation. Our study will begin with customary covenant practices so that you will be able to recognize these statements. Your ultimate goal through studying this series is to become covenant-minded. This will, in turn, strengthen your commitments to your family, friends and business associates. But most importantly, it will strengthen your faith in God.

Blood covenants are recorded in all ancient civilizations. Only the relatively recent societies have done away with this practice. Covenant agreements were entered into to bind two tribes together. The grounds for this union were always based on their differences, not their similarities.

> *The grounds for [covenant agreements] were always based on their differences, not their similarities.*

(You will notice that this is exactly the opposite of man's natural tendency apart from covenant relationship. Racism and denomination-alism, which are in direct opposition to the purpose of covenant agreements, are perfect examples. These beliefs cause a separation between

those who are different either because of skin color or religious prefer-
ences. They separate men who are different and bind together men who are
similar. The problem with this is that you not only have the same strengths,
but you also have the same weaknesses. So, in the end, you're left with
nothing to save you from your weaknesses.)

In ancient civilizations, since the covenant agreement was entered
based on *differences* and not similarities, their strengths and weaknesses
balanced each other out. This union made both tribes strong.

Lengthy discussions were made in order to produce agreement and
harmony. During these negotiations, the two families agreed to each party's
responsibility in the union. They agreed upon a blessing for keeping the
terms, as well as a curse for breaking them. The fear of the curse and the
desire to benefit from the blessings kept the parties in line.

Then each family chose a representative. The representative was one
who had the very character of the family. If the family were strong war-
riors, the representative was the greatest and most highly skilled warrior of
them all. If the family were business-minded, the representative was the
shrewdest business person in the family. The representative was always
someone with whom the whole family could identify. He was also someone
with whom outsiders identified the family.

> *In our covenant
> with God,
> Jesus is our
> representative....*

(In our covenant with God, Jesus is our
representative, and the phrases in the Pauline
Epistles which state, "in Christ," "in Whom,"
"in Him," "through Christ," are statements of
our identification with Him. As a born-again
believer, you have taken on His nature and character. Thus, you are identified as a Christian or
"little Christ.")

Next, they chose a covenant site. It was a
place where all the family members could gather
around to watch the covenant rite take place.

After the site was chosen, the sacrificial animals were selected. They were most often large animals who would shed a great deal of blood when slaughtered. The animals were cut from the back of the neck down the backbone. The two halves fell to the ground, laying opposite of each other. Their blood spilled on the ground between the two halves, and the alley between them was customarily called the walkway of blood.

As the covenant ceremony began, each representative removed his coat and exchanged it with the other representative. The coat represented the strength and authority of each family. By exchanging coats, they symbolically exchanged authority. Then they exchanged their weapons belts, which meant they would fight one another's battles.

(Ephesians 6, where the Bible talks about putting on the whole armor of God, is a covenant statement. He has given us His armor and joined forces with us to fight our enemy, the devil.)

After the exchange of coats and weapons belts, the representatives stated the terms of the covenant. Then the participants performed the walk of blood. They walked between the two animal halves and stood in the midst of the blood. They made irrevocable promises and stated the curse or penalty for breaking the promises.

This part of the covenant rite was very impressive. The sight, smell and feel of blood is an awesome thing, not easily forgotten. Covenants were cut and blood was shed so the promises would make a deep and lasting impression on the memories of each of the family members.

Also a very impressive procedure, the covenant representatives then cut themselves either on the wrist or the hand in order to mingle their blood together. This signified that the two were actually one, having the same blood. They lifted their arms so everyone could see the cuts. Then they swore oaths by their gods. Gunpowder or another substance was rubbed into the cut to make the scar that much more outstanding. The purpose of this procedure was to affect the memories of the families. That awesome, ugly scar would forever remind them of the promises they had made to each other.

Then the two families exchanged their names. Actually, they joined their names together. For example, if the Williamses and the Burgs made covenant together, from that moment on they were known as the Williamsburgs. In exchanging their names, they also exchanged their friendship.

Then came a covenant meal of bread and wine. This was the grand finale of the covenant rite. The bread represented the body, and the wine represented the blood. The meal of bread and wine symbolized each family giving themselves to the other family, even to the point of dying for one another if need be. They ate "in remembrance" of what they did that day in cutting a covenant together. ᴄᴥ

Now Begin Enjoying It

Does this remind you of Jesus? At the Last Supper, He said "...this is my body, which is broken for you: this do in remembrance of me....This cup is the new testament in my blood: this do ye, as oft as you drink it, in remembrance of me" (1 Corinthians 11:24-25). You see, the Bible is a book of covenants. And there is a reason behind every symbol and phrase in it. As we continue our study, your covenant with God will come more and more into focus, and your faith will become stronger than ever.

Tape/CD 1 Outlined

I. Purpose of covenant agreements
   A. To bind two or more families together
   B. To unite in both strengths and weaknesses

II. Covenant practices
   A. Come to terms of agreement
       1. Promises
       2. Blessing
       3. Curse
   B. Representatives chosen
   C. Site chosen
   D. Covenant rite
       1. Terms stated
       2. Blessing stated
       3. Curse stated

III. We enter the second covenant by
   A. Faith in the blood of Jesus
   B. Becoming His joint-heir

Study Questions

(1) What was the purpose of entering into a covenant agreement with another tribe or family? _____

_____

_____

_____

(2) What was the basis for the union? _____

_____

_____

_____

(3) Why was there a blessing and a curse involved in making a covenant?

_____

_____

_____

(4) In your own words, explain how a covenant union differs from the natural tendency of man to unite with another man or group. Use school cliques, racism, or denominationalism to illustrate. _____

_____

_____

_____

_____

(5) Personal application: How do you expect to benefit from studying this series on the covenant? _____

_____

_____

_____

Study Notes

"I the Lord have called thee in righteousness, and will hold
thine hand, and will keep thee, and give thee for a covenant
of the people, for a light of the Gentiles."
Isaiah 42:6

"And it came to pass...that the soul of Jonathan was knit with the soul of David, and Jonathan loved him as his own soul. Then Jonathan and David made a covenant, because he loved him as his own soul."

1 Samuel 18:1, 3

Because of your covenant with God, nothing

you do can separate you from His love.

TAPE/CD TWO
Covenant Relationships

God's Love Is Not Based on What You Deserve, but on What He's Promised

Establishing a
Loyal Relationship

FOCUS: "For God so loved the world, that he gave his only begotten Son, that whosoever believeth in him should not perish, but have everlasting life" (John 3:16).

The purpose of a covenant is to establish a relationship which is impossible to break. The covenant has procedures and customs which guarantee the relationship. It has both a curse to discourage breaking the relationship and a blessing to encourage loyalty. Establishing a covenant agreement is the closest man can come to attaining the degree of God's loyalty.

In God's covenant, His motivation for keeping His Word is His love, not the fear of a curse. His integrity is completely dependent on His own character. God's love entails a loyalty that is true even toward those who are disloyal to Him. In other words, God is faithful to His Word even when we are unfaithful to Him.

In God's covenant, His motivation for keeping His Word is His love.

The quality of God's love is difficult for human nature to understand. Human love without a covenant always has a self-preservation and self-protection quality about it. Human love is never totally unselfish apart from a covenant. It can never completely give of itself for fear of being hurt. But God's love gives and gives even when nothing is given in return.

The Hebrew word for God's love is *hesed*. Its New Testament Greek equivalent is *agape*. There is no definition for this word, *hesed*, but its meaning comes to light as you receive a revelation of a covenant relationship. Translators have had a hard time translating this word into English. It has been translated as "loving-kindness" and as "mercy," but these words are a far cry from its full meaning. *Hesed* means "unending loyalty with all of its implications." *Hesed* means that no matter what happens and no matter how little we give to Him in return, we will forever be at the forefront of God's thinking. Nothing will take precedence over His devotion toward us and His concern for our welfare.

According to John 3:16, it was *hesed* that motivated God to send Jesus as the Lamb slain for our sins. "For God so loved the world, that he gave his only begotten Son, that whosoever believeth in him should not perish, but have everlasting life." His body is marked with the remembrance of that love. The marks are the nail scars on His hands and feet. They are the scars on His head, in His side, and on His back. He can never forget us nor the price He paid to redeem us. He has made Himself to be one with us. He has knit His soul and His Spirit with ours. ✍

A Demonstration of Covenant

✍ **FOCUS:** "And it came to pass, when he had made an end of speaking unto Saul, that the soul of Jonathan was knit with the soul of David, and Jonathan loved him as his own soul. Then Jonathan and David made a covenant, because he loved him as his own soul" (1 Samuel 18:1, 3).

This is the kind of loyalty David and Jonathan shared. The Bible says in 1 Samuel 18:1, "And it came to pass, when he had made an end of speaking unto Saul, that the soul of Jonathan was knit with the soul of David, and Jonathan loved him as his own soul." David and Jonathan had made a covenant with each other (1 Samuel 18:3). Their bond was so close it was as if they were one man, not two. Nothing could destroy or diminish the loyalty they had toward one another.

As you read further into David's story in 2 Samuel, you discover that through the years Saul, the king of Israel, developed an offense toward David. His bitterness led him to pollute his household with fear and lies about David. He believed David was out to steal his throne and take his life, so he spread these lies every way he could to whoever would listen. But Saul was deceived. David was the only truly loyal man he had in his kingdom. He was loyal because of his covenant with Jonathan.

In his fear and bitterness, Saul pursued David to kill him, and though David defended himself, his loyalty was never divided between the covenant and his own self-preservation. The covenant came first. He was so loyal that he cried out in 2 Samuel 9:1, "Is there yet any that is left of the house of Saul, that I may shew him kindness for Jonathan's sake?" The word *kindness* does not do justice to what David was actually saying. The Hebrew word is *hesed*. The mentality of this love is not just kindness. It is practically desperation to demonstrate undying loyalty no matter what happens to destroy the relationship. Even though Saul was trying to kill David and had even turned his whole household against him, David only wanted to be loyal.

> *God's love gives and gives even when nothing is given in return.*

Saul had made everyone believe that David wanted to kill them all. Everyone was in such fear over David's supposed threat to take over the throne, they were running for their lives. A maid grabbed a young boy, but in the rush she dropped him. He became a paraplegic as a result of the injuries he suffered in the fall.

At the point that David cried, "Is there anyone left of the house of Saul, to whom I may show *hesed* for Jonathan's sake?" he learned of this paralyzed boy who was the only heir left. David sent for him so that he could fulfill his covenant loyalty. This boy had been brainwashed into thinking that David wanted to kill him, but all David wanted to do was to love him for Jonathan's sake. He said, "Fear not: for I will surely show thee *hesed* for Jonathan thy father's sake. I will restore thee all the land of Saul thy father, and thou shalt eat bread at my table continually" (2 Samuel 9:7).

David's loyalty to Jonathan did not end when Jonathan died. It continued for several generations after him. This young boy did absolutely nothing to deserve the love he received from David. David's love was motivated by his covenant loyalty—nothing else. He was so driven by this loyalty he spent his energy in hot pursuit of someone with whom he was in covenant so he could demonstrate it. ⌗

Now Begin Enjoying It

When you see the depth of loyalty in a covenant relationship, you begin to understand God's loyalty and devotion to you. His love toward you and the blessings He bestows on you are not based on your conduct. They are based strictly on His overwhelming desire to love and to give. God is in hot pursuit of you so He can bestow His love and blessings on you.

❧ *Tape/CD 2 Outlined* ❧

I. Purpose of covenant
   A. To establish an unbreakable relationship
   B. Guaranteed by a blessing and a curse

II. God's covenant
   A. Guaranteed by *hesed* loving-kindness
      (unending loyalty)
   B. Reason for sending Jesus

III. David and Jonathan's covenant
   A. Unending loyalty
   B. Inseparable unity and undying loyalty
   C. Extended beyond Jonathan's death to his
      descendants

Study Questions

(1) What is the purpose of establishing a covenant? _____

_____

_____

_____

(2) What is God's motivation for keeping His Word? _____

_____

_____

_____

(3) Explain what **hesed** means. _____

_____

_____

_____

_____

(4) Compare God's loyalty to us with David's loyalty to Jonathan. ____

_____

_____

_____

_____

(5) Personal application: How has your perception of God's love for you changed since you have studied this message? _____

_____

_____

_____

_____

Study Notes

"But God commendeth his love toward us, in that,
while we were yet sinners, Christ died for us."
Romans 5:8

3

"Be strong and of a good courage,
fear not, nor be afraid of them: for the
Lord thy God, he it is that doth go
with thee; he will not fail thee, nor
forsake thee. And the Lord, he it is
that doth go before thee; he will be with
thee, he will not fail thee, neither forsake
thee: fear not, neither be dismayed."

Deuteronomy 31:6, 8

God reached out to you, making you an

heir to all of the blessing of God.

TAPE/CD THREE
Covenant Faith

God's Covenant Breaks the Curse—You Are No Longer Subject to It

Heirs of the Covenant

FOCUS: "Be strong and of a good courage, fear not, nor be afraid of them: for the Lord thy God, he it is that doth go with thee; he will not fail thee, nor forsake thee. And the Lord, he it is that doth go before thee; he will be with thee, he will not fail thee, neither forsake thee: fear not, neither be dismayed" (Deuteronomy 31:6, 8).

Another reason for studying our covenant is the direct effect it has on our faith. Many in the Body of Christ have said we are not meant to arbitrarily stand on a promise for a situation in our lives. They believe if God doesn't give it to you, then faith cannot produce the end result. Those who believe this way do not understand that God has entered into a covenant with us *specifically* so we will believe and trust the integrity of His promises. Understanding covenant relationships removes doubt as to whether God wants us to take His promises and stand on them.

Those who do understand the covenant know that God is *eager* to keep His Word. The covenant is at the forefront of His thinking all the time. And just to be sure the promises will mean as much to us as they do to God, He has told us to keep His Word in the center of our hearts and ever before our eyes. He has told us to meditate on it day and night, talk about it, and think on it continually.

> *Those who do understand the covenant know that God is eager to keep His Word.*

Deuteronomy 30 was written to the heirs of the covenant God made with Abraham, to give them an unchangeable written statement of God's will for them and His desire to bless them. He was telling His people that He didn't want them to live under a curse. He wanted them to be blessed, so He told them how they could be.

To be blessed, they had to come out from under the curse. When man fell, God cursed Satan (Genesis 3:14-15), but because the Fall separated the human race from God and joined it to the devil, man came under the curse of his new god—Satan. To enter the covenant with God meant that they were brought out from under the curse. If they would walk in His ways, they could avoid the curse and be blessed.

"Walking in His ways" had more than one meaning. It meant that God wanted them to keep His statutes and obey His commandments. But it also meant walking in the "way of blood" between the animal halves. The way of blood was the most impressive part of the covenant rite. It was the part that left an indelible mark in the minds of the covenant partners. ᔕ᙮

Reaching Out to Us

FOCUS: "Having therefore, brethren, boldness to enter into the holiest by the blood of Jesus, By a new and living way, which he hath consecrated for us, through the veil, that is to say, his flesh" (Hebrews 10: 19-20).

For us, as New Covenant believers, we have a new way of living according to Hebrews 10:20. And we can not only walk in the ways *of* God, we walk in the way *with* God. We walk through the passover portals of the blood of the Lamb that was shed for our sins. That blood is at the forefront of God's thinking. It represents His undying loyalty toward us. It is what Jesus meant when He said "I will never leave you or forsake you." It is what God said in Deuteronomy 31:6, 8. "Be strong and of a good courage, fear not, nor be afraid of them: for the Lord thy God, he it is that doth go with thee; he will not fail thee, nor forsake thee. And the Lord, he it is that doth go before thee; he will be with thee, he will not fail thee, neither forsake thee: fear not, neither be dismayed." We have nothing to fear, no matter what happens, because God's loyalty toward us will never fail.

> *And we can not only walk in the ways of God, we walk in the way with God.*

All through the Old Testament, God was trying to get across to His people how much He loved them and how desperately He wanted to bless them. God's *hesed* drove Him to find a way to convey this intense desire to them. The method He chose to convey this message was to cut a covenant with a man named Abram. Since covenants were customary at that time, Abram was very familiar with the covenant agreement.

Until then, Abram had worshiped the moon and the stars—gods which never reached out to do anything for him. And suddenly, the Almighty God reached down from heaven and promised to bless him and to make him the father of many nations. At that time, Abram was an old man and his wife, Sarai, was old and barren. It was very difficult for Abram to believe that God was able—and willing—to do this favor for him. Cutting a covenant was the most convincing way God could affect Abram's faith.

The covenant is recorded in Genesis 15, 16, 17 and 18, and while the covenant rite did not take place at one time in one place, it included all of the customs of the day. The sacrificial animals were a heifer, a she goat, a ram, a turtle-dove and a pigeon. The animals were split down the back. A way of blood was paved between the halves. Abram and God exchanged names, promises were made, and a blessing and a curse were pronounced. The scar of the covenant was the circumcision of every man child. And through the covenant, God conveyed the message that He had joined Himself in an irrevocable union with Abraham and all of his descendants, for one reason: to bless them. ❦

Now Begin Enjoying It

You have a New Covenant with better promises. When you study covenant enough to get a revelation of it, you can become as fully persuaded of God's desire to fulfill His promises to you as Abraham was. This will, in turn, have a direct effect on your faith in God and the promises He has made to you!

~ *Tape/CD 3 Outlined* ~

I. Purpose of the Covenant
   A. To strengthen our faith in God's loyalty
   B. To strengthen our faith in God's desire to bless us

II. Results of the covenant
   A. Established relationship between God and man
   B. Brought blessing to man

III. Rite of the covenant
   A. Sacrificial animal
   B. Way of blood
   C. Names exchanged
   D. Blessing and curse
   E. Promises sworn
   F. Scar
   G. Covenant meal

Study Questions

(1) To whom is the book of Deuteronomy written? Why? _____

_____

_____

_____

_____

_____

(2) What does the blood of Jesus represent to the Father? _____

_____

_____

_____

_____

(3) God chose to cut a covenant with Abraham in order to convince him of His desire to bless him. Why did God choose this method? _____

_____

_____

_____

_____

_____

(4) Personal application: How can you become fully persuaded of God's desire to bless you?_____

_____

_____

_____

_____

Study Notes

"And if ye be Christ's, then are ye Abraham's seed,
and heirs according to the promise."
Galatians 3:29

4

"Christ hath redeemed us from the curse of the law, being made a curse for us: for it is written, Cursed is every one that hangeth on a tree: That the blessing of Abraham might come on the Gentiles through Jesus Christ; that we might receive the promise of the Spirit through faith."

Galatians 3:13-14

Through Jesus' sacrifice, you are free to enter the presence of God. You are free from any sin or hindrance that would keep you out of His presence. You are FREE!

TAPE/CD FOUR
Hesed/Agape Love

God's Love and His Loyalty Cannot be Separated

The New Covenant

FOCUS: "Christ hath redeemed us from the curse of the law, being made a curse for us: for it is written, Cursed is every one that hangeth on a tree: That the blessing of Abraham might come on the Gentiles through Jesus Christ; that we might receive the promise of the Spirit through faith" (Galatians 3:13-14).

Studying the covenant will enable you to grasp an understanding of God's love. Apart from the covenant, there is no way to comprehend how loyal God is to His Word, and God's loyalty and His love cannot be separated. Communicating the depth of His love and loyalty in a way that man's finite mind could grasp was so difficult that God chose a covenant as the means to convey His commitment.

A covenant is the most serious and binding commitment a man can make with another man. The loyalty between covenant partners is stronger than the loyalty between siblings. That is why it is so hard to comprehend God's love apart from the covenant.

God's response to the fall of man is a perfect example of His intense love and loyalty to mankind. When Adam sinned and joined himself to the devil, he lost his ability to comprehend and fellowship with God. God immediately put into motion His plan of redemption. That plan ultimately meant the Son of God shedding His own blood. In his fallen state, man would never be able to understand love to

> *God joined Himself to man in a covenant in order to make His strength, His authority, His name, His weapons and His power available to man.*

that degree. God had to lead man step-by-step to the place where he could understand it. It started with man shedding his own blood through circumcision as a sign of the covenant.

God knew that the basis of a covenant union was differences. Two families would recognize each other's weaknesses and each other's strengths. They would decide to join together in a covenant and balance out those strengths and weaknesses. In other words, where one family was strong, the other was weak. Together, they were both strong. God joined Himself to man in a covenant in order to make His strength, His authority, His Name, His weapons, and His power available to man. He joined Himself in a covenant in order to make a way to pour out His blessings on mankind.

The first covenant was with Abraham. It had a curse with it because Abraham was human and capable of breaking the terms of the covenant. The second covenant was with Jesus. He is incapable of breaking the terms of the covenant, and therefore, this covenant has no need for a curse. Galatians 3:13-14 says that Jesus redeemed us from the curse by bearing it for us so the blessing of Abraham might come on the Gentiles through faith.

We enter the second covenant by becoming joint-heirs with Jesus when we are born again. In this covenant, Jesus is not only the covenant partner with God the Father, He also became the covenant sacrifice. He is the Lamb slain for our sins. His blood shed is the new and living way we have to enter the presence of God. His body is marked with the scars of the covenant. He is also our

> *We enter the second covenant by becoming joint-heirs with Jesus when we are born again.*

covenant representative—the only Mediator between God and man. He has given us His Name. He has given us His weapons. He has given us His identity. He has even become the covenant meal. ເ໑

Now Begin Enjoying It

Can you see the intensity of God's *hesed* in desiring to bring blessing to you? The first covenant opened the door to the second covenant. And in the second covenant, God has taken *all* of the responsibility of keeping it. You are blessed because of Jesus' faithfulness, not yours. You don't have to do anything to earn God's love and blessing. He gives it because it is His nature to give. Through establishing the covenant, He simply made a way to give it. All you have to do is be the recipient of it through faith in the *hesed* and grace of God.

❧ *Tape/CD 4 Outlined* ❧

I. The fall of man
  A. Separated man from God
  B. Left man with no understanding of God's love

II. God's response to the Fall
  A. Plan of redemption
  B. Restoration of covenant relationship
    1. Covenant made with Abraham
    2. Covenant made with Jesus

III. We enter the second covenant by
  A. Faith in the blood of Jesus
  B. Becoming His joint-heir

✎ *Study Questions* ✎

(1) What is the most serious commitment a man could ever make with another man? _____

_____

_____

_____

_____

(2) Why did God join Himself to man in a covenant relationship? _____

_____

_____

_____

_____

(3) Compare the Abrahamic covenant with our covenant and explain why there is no need for a curse in ours. _____

_____

_____

_____

_____

*(4) Personal application: How has a revelation of **hesed/agape** changed you?* _____

_____

_____

_____

_____

Study Notes

"*Being justified freely by his grace through the redemption that is in Christ Jesus: Whom God hath set forth to be a propitiation through faith in his blood, to declare his righteousness for the remission of sins that are past, through the forbearance of God.*"

Romans 3:24-25

5

"Bless the Lord, O my soul, and forget not all his benefits... who crowneth thee with lovingkindness and tender mercies."

Psalms 103: 2, 4

Through Jesus, God has blessed you.

He has *empowered you to prosper—*

spirit, soul and body!

TAPE/CD FIVE
Hesed—The Power of God

Because of His Love,
God's Covenant
Provides Everything
You Will Ever Need

Paving the Way

FOCUS: "Now the promises (covenants, agreements) were decreed and made to Abraham and his Seed (his Offspring, his Heir). He [God] does not say, And to seeds (descendants, heirs), as if referring to many persons, but, And to your Seed (your Descendant, your Heir), obviously referring to one individual, Who is [none other than] Christ (the Messiah)" (Galatians 3:16, *The Amplified Bible*).

Genesis 15, 16, 17 and 18 record God's covenant as He cut it with Abraham. Nothing was left out of this covenant. Every aspect of the manmade covenants of Abraham's day was included. The purpose of this covenant was to bind God to Abraham and His descendants in an unbreakable bond. It was also to convince Abraham of the intensity of God's desire to bring blessing to him and of His unwavering loyalty. Cutting the covenant was the only way that God could convince man of His *hesed*. God didn't cut the covenant with Abram because *He* needed it. He did it to convince Abram of His love and desire to bless him.

In the New Covenant, Jesus became everything for us.

In cutting this covenant with Abraham, God was paving the way for His ultimate blessing—Jesus. When God said, "I am the God of Abraham," He didn't mean just that He was God *over* Abraham. Of course, it did mean this, but it also meant that God would be born of Abraham's seed. "I am the God of Abraham" meant "I am Christ" (Galatians 3:16), "Son of Man." The covenant with Abraham was the inroad to bring Jesus into the earth as the Messiah.

The covenant with Abraham was God's way of uniting man with God and God with man. The Old Covenant was not enough. It merely foreshadowed the New Covenant. In the New Covenant, Jesus became *everything* for us. He was the sacrificial Lamb. His blood was shed. He was and is our Representative. He has sworn by Himself because there is no one greater to swear by. He has promised to bless us, and He has even taken the curse for us. He has given us His strength, His authority, and His weapons. And He's given Himself as our covenant meal. ✑

The Ultimate Blessing

✐ **FOCUS:** "For I am not ashamed of the gospel of Christ: for it is the power of God unto salvation to every one that believeth; to the Jew first, and also to the Greek" (Romans 1:16).

Jesus is the statement of God's *hesed*—His forgiveness, His loyalty, His devotion and everything that God is. Nehemiah 9:17 says, "But thou art a God ready to pardon, gracious and merciful, slow to anger, and of great kindness, and forsookest them not." Because of His *hesed,* God was ready to pardon before man ever sinned. Because of His *hesed,* God had predetermined that if man broke *his* bond with Him, He would not break His bond with man. His desire to bring blessing would continue.

To *bless* means "to empower one to prosper." In bringing blessing to us through Jesus, God empowers us to prosper in spirit, soul, and body. Because of His *hesed,* God's covenant will provide everything that we could ever need—spirit, soul, or body. In Psalm 103:1-8, the Bible says,

> Bless the Lord, O my soul: and all that is within me, bless his
> holy name. Bless the Lord, O my soul, and forget not all his
> benefits: Who forgiveth all thine iniquities; who healeth all
> thy diseases; Who redeemeth thy life from destruction; who

crowneth thee with lovingkindness and tender mercies; Who satisfieth thy mouth with good things; so that thy youth is renewed like the eagle's. The Lord executeth righteousness and judgment for all that are oppressed. He made known his ways unto Moses, his acts unto the children of Israel. The Lord is merciful and gracious, slow to anger, and plenteous in mercy.

These verses are a statement of what *hesed* will do. God made the covenant because He is looking for someone to whom He can bestow His blessings and use His power to deliver. He is desperately looking for a way to bless us.

Isaiah 54:8-9 is a further statement of God's *hesed*. "In a little wrath I hid my face from thee for a moment; but with everlasting kindness will I have mercy on thee, saith the Lord thy Redeemer. For this is as the waters of Noah unto me: for as I have sworn that the waters of Noah should no more go over the earth; so have I sworn that I would not be wroth with thee, nor rebuke thee." God punished Jesus for man's disobedience. He is looking for a way to bless man, not a way to rebuke and punish man. This is what the covenant is all about.

> *Jesus is the statement of God's hesed— His forgiveness, His loyalty, His devotion and everything that God is.*

Galatians 3:6-8 says that the covenant is the gospel, and Romans 1:16 says the gospel is the power of God. Therefore *hesed* is the power of God because the covenant is the demonstration of *hesed*. God has not only demonstrated His *hesed* toward us, but through Jesus, He has filled us with His own *hesed*. Why? So that we may be demonstrators of His love toward one another. ❦

Now Begin Enjoying It

We have been commanded to love one another as He has loved us (John 15:12). In the New Testament, the Greek counterpart of *hesed* is *agape*. To translate these words as "love"

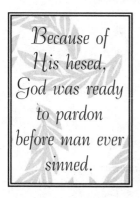

Because of His hesed, God was ready to pardon before man ever sinned.

falls far too short of what these words mean. *Hesed/agape* is a statement of the motivation behind everything God has ever done for mankind. It is a statement of His power in creating the world as a home for His beloved family to enjoy. It is a statement of His power in bringing redemption after man sinned. *Hesed/agape* is a statement of His power in sending us the Holy Spirit. He loves you so much that He did not leave you to love others without giving you His capacity with which to do it. He has given you His own *hesed*, shed abroad in your hearts by the Holy Ghost to enable and empower you to love as He loves. That revelation in itself is a statement of what *hesed/agape* is.

Tape/CD 5 Outlined

I. The Abrahamic covenant
   A. God's method of bringing blessing
   B. God's method of bringing Jesus

II. Jesus
   A. God's *hesed*
   B. Forgiveness
   C. Blessing
   D. Redemption from the curse

III. Our response
   A. To love God
   B. To love one another

Study Questions

(1) How was the covenant with Abraham the inroad to bringing Jesus into the earth as the Messiah? _____

_____

_____

_____

(2) Explain Jesus' complete role in the New Covenant. _____

_____

_____

_____

(3) Explain why is Jesus a statement of God's **hesed**. _____

_____

_____

_____

_____

(4) What motivates God to meet all of our needs? _____

_____

_____

_____

(5) Personal application: How has God enabled you to love others? ___

_____

_____

_____

Study Notes

"But God commendeth his love toward us, in that, while we were yet sinners, Christ died for us."
Romans 5:8

6

"Charity suffereth long, and is kind; charity envieth not; charity vaunteth not itself, is not puffed up, Doth not behave itself unseemly, seeketh not her own, is not easily provoked, thinketh no evil; Rejoiceth not in iniquity, but rejoiceth in the truth; Beareth all things, believeth all things, hopeth all things, endureth all things. Charity never faileth...."

1 Corinthians 13:4-8

You are a child of God, and because of that relationship, you are an example of His love everywhere you go.

You Can Have God's Love and Devotion in All of Your Relationships

An Example of Agape

FOCUS: "And so faith, hope, love abide [faith—conviction and belief respecting man's relation to God and divine things; hope—joyful and confident expectation of eternal salvation; love—true affection for God and man, growing out of God's love for and in us], these three; but the greatest of these is love" (I Corinthians 13:13, *The Amplified Bible*).

The covenant is God's means of supplying every need we could ever have. Our first need is to have our relationship reestablished with the Father. This is done through faith in the blood of Jesus that was shed for our sins. Once we receive Jesus as our Lord and Savior, our relationship with the Father is secured—we have peace with our Maker. God's purpose in forgiving us is that we abound in His peace.

In this New Covenant, the word *agape* (the New Testament counterpart to *hesed*) is tied to His grace and mercy. The grace and mercy of God in the New Covenant introduce God's compassion. His compassion means that God is merciful to the point that even when our loyalty fails, our Blood Brother, Jesus, has *hesed/agape* mercy and grace and forgives us when we confess our failure. His *hesed/agape* protects us, and He doesn't even let the Father know that we have failed. He is our Advocate with the Father and through *hesed/agape* maintains our peace with Him!

Once we establish our peace with the Father, we are to maintain our peace with one another. Jesus commanded that we love one another as He has

> *We cannot separate ourselves from those in the Body of Christ who are different.*

loved us. We must look at each other in a different light once we understand the covenant. The covenant was cut based on people's differences, not their similarities. Now that we understand covenant, we cannot separate ourselves from those in the Body of Christ who are different. Those very differences are what bind us together through the blood of Jesus. The Scripture says that we are fitly joined together by every joint supplying its part (Ephesians 4:16). If we serve the Head of the Body, we cannot ignore serving the Body. We may be different, but we are all one. Why? Because we have obtained peace with the Father through the blood of Jesus. ❧

Maintaining the Agape

FOCUS: "But by the grace of God I am what I am: and his grace which was bestowed upon me was not in vain; but I laboured more abundantly than they all: yet not I, but the grace of God which was with me" (1 Corinthians 15:10).

First Corinthians 13:1-3 tells us that any service we render that is not motivated by God's *hesed/agape* is done for nought. Then, verses 4-8 are the test of our motivation. *Hesed/agape* suffers long and is kind; *hesed/agape* does not parade itself, is not puffed up; does not behave rudely, does not seek its own, is not provoked, thinks no evil; does not rejoice in iniquity, but rejoices in the truth; bears all things, believes all things, hopes all things, endures all things. *Hesed/agape* never fails. When these are your motives in all things, not only will you keep your peace with God, but you will maintain peace with others.

How can we maintain this quality of love? It is by God's own love shed abroad in our hearts. The Apostle Paul knew this well. He said, "For I am the least of the apostles, that am not meet to be called an apostle, because I persecuted the church of God. But by the grace of God I am what I am: and his grace which was bestowed upon me was not in vain; but I laboured more abundantly than they all: yet not I, but the grace of God which was with me" (1 Corinthians 15:9-10). When Paul said he was who he was because of the grace of God and that he labored because of the grace of God, it was God's own *hesed/agape* coming on him to lay down his life for his brethren's sake. Grace, love and mercy are all tied together in the New Covenant.

As you study the book of Philippians, you find that the only reason Paul didn't choose to go home to be with the Lord was so that he could minister to his brethren. What love! Only God's love in him, on him and coming out of him could enable him to be so unselfish. ✑

Now Begin Enjoying It

You have the same love of God shed abroad in your heart that Paul had. What will cause this kind of love to flow out of you? A revelation of the covenant. His grace abounding toward you in *hesed/agape* is sufficient. Once you see that God is desperately seeking a way to convince man of His love for him, and you see the length He went to reestablish His relationship with man, your whole life revolves around ministering God's love to others. With a revelation of the covenant, your love and devotion toward others is not based on how well they perform. It is based on *hesed/agape* which keeps loving and stays loyal even when others have stopped.

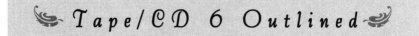

Tape/CD 6 Outlined

I. Covenant peace
   A. Peace with God through forgiveness of sins
   B. Peace with man through *hesed/agape*

II. Commandment
   A. Love as Jesus loved
   B. Equipped by God

III. How God's love responds
   A. Suffers long and is kind
   B. Does not parade itself, is not puffed up
   C. Does not behave rudely or seek its own
   D. Is not provoked, thinks no evil
   E. Does not rejoice in iniquity, but truth
   F. Bears, believes, hopes and endures all things
   G. Never fails

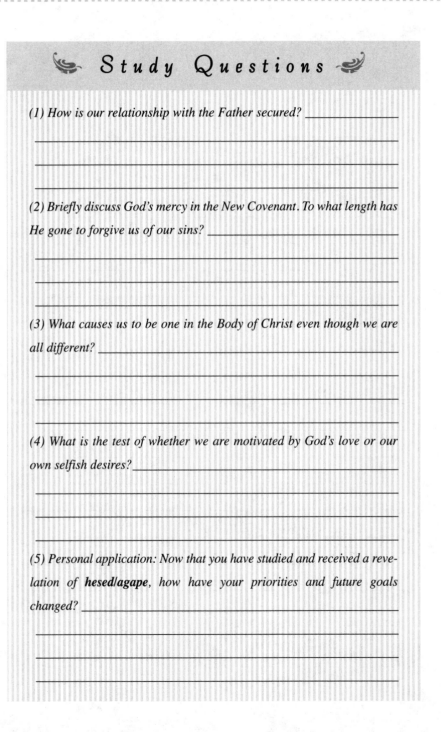

Study Questions

(1) How is our relationship with the Father secured? _____

_____

_____

_____

(2) Briefly discuss God's mercy in the New Covenant. To what length has He gone to forgive us of our sins? _____

_____

_____

_____

(3) What causes us to be one in the Body of Christ even though we are all different? _____

_____

_____

_____

*(4) What is the test of whether we are motivated by God's love or our own selfish desires?*_____

_____

_____

_____

*(5) Personal application: Now that you have studied and received a revelation of **hesed/agape**, how have your priorities and future goals changed?* _____

_____

_____

_____

Study Notes

Prayer for Salvation and Baptism in the Holy Spirit

Heavenly Father, I come to You in the Name of Jesus. Your Word says, "Whosoever shall call on the name of the Lord shall be saved" (Acts 2:21). I am calling on You. I pray and ask Jesus to come into my heart and be Lord over my life according to Romans 10:9-10. "If thou shalt confess with thy mouth the Lord Jesus, and shalt believe in thine heart that God hath raised him from the dead, thou shalt be saved. For with the heart man believeth unto righteousness; and with the mouth confession is made unto salvation." I do that now. I confess that Jesus is Lord, and I believe in my heart that God raised Him from the dead.

I am now reborn! I am a Christian—a child of Almighty God! I am saved! You also said in Your Word, "If ye then, being evil, know how to give good gifts unto your children: HOW MUCH MORE shall your heavenly Father give the Holy Spirit to them that ask him?" (Luke 11:13). I'm also asking You to fill me with the Holy Spirit. Holy Spirit, rise up within me as I praise God. I fully expect to speak with other tongues as You give me the utterance (Acts 2:4). In Jesus' Name. Amen!

Begin to praise God for filling you with the Holy Spirit. Speak those words and syllables you receive—not in your own language, but the language given to you by the Holy Spirit. You have to use your own voice. God will not force you to speak. Don't be concerned with how it sounds. It is a heavenly language!

Continue with the blessing God has given you and pray in the spirit every day.

You are a born-again, Spirit-filled believer. You'll never be the same!

Find a good church that boldly preaches God's Word and obeys it. Become a part of a church family who will love and care for you as you love and care for them.

We need to be connected to each other. It increases our strength in God. It's God's plan for us.

Make it a habit to watch the *Believer's Voice of Victory* television broadcast and become a doer of the Word, who is blessed in his doing (James 1:22-25).

About the Author

Kenneth Copeland is co-founder and president of Kenneth Copeland Ministries in Fort Worth, Texas, and best-selling author of books that include *Managing God's Mutual Funds—Yours and His, How to Discipline Your Flesh* and *Honor—Walking in Honesty, Truth and Integrity.*

Now in his 35th year as a minister of the gospel of Christ and teacher of God's Word, Kenneth is the recording artist of such award-winning albums as his Grammy nominated *Only the Redeemed, In His Presence, He Is Jehovah* and his most recently released *Just a Closer Walk.* He also co-stars as the character Wichita Slim in the children's adventure videos *The Gunslinger, Covenant Rider* and the movie *The Treasure of Eagle Mountain,* and as Daniel Lyon in the *Commander Kellie and the Superkids*_{SM} videos *Armor of Light* and *Judgment: The Trial of Commander Kellie.*

With the help of offices and staff in the United States, Canada, England, Australia, South Africa and Ukraine, Kenneth is fulfilling his vision to boldly preach the uncompromised Word of God from the top of this world, to the bottom, and all the way around. His ministry reaches millions of people worldwide through daily and Sunday TV broadcasts, magazines, teaching tapes and videos, conventions and campaigns, and the World Wide Web.

Learn more about
Kenneth Copeland Ministries
by visiting our Web site at
www.kcm.org

Books Available From
Kenneth Copeland Ministries

by Kenneth Copeland

*   A Ceremony of Marriage
        A Matter of Choice
        Covenant of Blood
        Faith and Patience—The Power Twins
*   Freedom From Fear
        Giving and Receiving
        Honor—Walking in Honesty, Truth and Integrity
        How to Conquer Strife
        How to Discipline Your Flesh
        How to Receive Communion
        In Love There Is No Fear
        Know Your Enemy
        Living at the End of Time—A Time of
               Supernatural Increase
        Love Never Fails
        Managing God's Mutual Funds—Yours and His
        Mercy—The Divine Rescue of the Human Race
*   Now Are We in Christ Jesus
        One Nation Under God (gift book with CD enclosed)
*   Our Covenant With God
        Partnership, Sharing the Vision—Sharing the Grace
*   Prayer—Your Foundation for Success
*   Prosperity: The Choice Is Yours
        Rumors of War
*   Sensitivity of Heart
*   Six Steps to Excellence in Ministry
*   Sorrow Not! Winning Over Grief and Sorrow
*   The Decision Is Yours
*   The Force of Faith
*   The Force of Righteousness
        The Image of God in You
        The Laws of Prosperity
*   The Mercy of God (Available in Spanish only)
        The Outpouring of the Spirit—The Result of Prayer
*   The Power of the Tongue
        The Power to Be Forever Free
*   The Winning Attitude

Turn Your Hurts Into Harvests
Walking in the Realm of the Miraculous
* Welcome to the Family
* You Are Healed!
Your Right-Standing With God

by Gloria Copeland

* And Jesus Healed Them All
Are You Listening?
Are You Ready?
Be a Vessel of Honor
Build Your Financial Foundation
Fight On!
Go With the Flow
God's Prescription for Divine Health
God's Success Formula
God's Will for You
God's Will for Your Healing
God's Will Is Prosperity
* God's Will Is the Holy Spirit
* Harvest of Health
Hidden Treasures
Living Contact
Living in Heaven's Blessings Now
* Love—The Secret to Your Success
No Deposit—No Return
Pleasing the Father
Pressing In—It's Worth It All
Shine On!
The Grace That Makes Us Holy
The Power to Live a New Life
The Protection of Angels
The Secret Place of God's Protection (gift book with CD enclosed)
The Unbeatable Spirit of Faith
* Walk in the Spirit (Available in Spanish only)
Walk With God
Well Worth the Wait
Words That Heal (gift book with CD enclosed)
Your Promise of Protection—The Power of
the 91st Psalm

Books Co-Authored by Kenneth and Gloria Copeland

Family Promises
Healing Promises
Prosperity Promises
Protection Promises

*   From Faith to Faith—A Daily Guide to Victory
From Faith to Faith—A Perpetual Calendar

One Word From God Series
• One Word From God Can Change Your Destiny
• One Word From God Can Change Your Family
• One Word From God Can Change Your Finances
• One Word From God Can Change Your Formula
   for Success
• One Word From God Can Change Your Health
• One Word From God Can Change Your Nation
• One Word From God Can Change Your
   Prayer Life
• One Word From God Can Change Your
   Relationships

Over The Edge—A Youth Devotional
Load Up—A Youth Devotional
Pursuit of His Presence—A Daily Devotional
Pursuit of His Presence—A Perpetual Calendar

Other Books Published by KCP

The First 30 Years—A Journey of Faith
   The story of the lives of Kenneth and
    Gloria Copeland.
Real People. Real Needs. Real Victories.
   A book of testimonies to encourage your faith.

John G. Lake—His Life, His Sermons, His
   Boldness of Faith

*Available in Spanish

The Holiest of All by Andrew Murray
The New Testament in Modern Speech
   by Richard Francis Weymouth
Unchained by Mac Gober

Products Designed for Today's Children and Youth

And Jesus Healed Them All (confession book and CD gift package)
Baby Praise Board Book
Baby Praise Christmas Board Book
Noah's Ark Coloring Book
The Best of *Shout!* Adventure Comics
The *Shout!* Giant Flip Coloring Book
The *Shout!* Joke Book
The *Shout!* Super-Activity Book
Wichita Slim's Campfire Stories

_Commander Kellie and the Superkids_SM Books:
The SWORD Adventure Book
*Commander Kellie and the Superkids*SM
Solve-It-Yourself Mysteries
*Commander Kellie and the Superkids*SM
Adventure Series: Middle Grade Novels by
Christopher P.N. Maselli

   #1 The Mysterious Presence
   #2 The Quest for the Second Half
   #3 Escape From Jungle Island
   #4 In Pursuit of the Enemy
   #5 Caged Rivalry
   #6 Mystery of the Missing Junk
   #7 Out of Breath
   #8 The Year Mashela Stole Christmas

*Available in Spanish

World Offices
of Kenneth Copeland Ministries

For more information about KCM and a free
catalog, please write the office nearest you:

Kenneth Copeland Ministries
Fort Worth, Texas 76192-0001

Kenneth Copeland
Locked Bag 2600
Mansfield Delivery Centre
QUEENSLAND 4122
AUSTRALIA

Kenneth Copeland
Post Office Box 15
BATH
BA1 3XN
U.K.

Kenneth Copeland
Private Bag X 909
FONTAINEBLEAU
2032
REPUBLIC OF SOUTH AFRICA

Kenneth Copeland
Post Office Box 378
Surrey, B.C.
V3T 5B6
CANADA

Kenneth Copeland Ministries
Post Office Box 84
L'VIV 79000
UKRAINE

We're Here for You!

Believer's Voice of Victory **Television Broadcast**

Join Kenneth and Gloria Copeland and the *Believer's Voice of Victory* broadcasts Monday through Friday and on Sunday each week, and learn how faith in God's Word can take your life from ordinary to extraordinary. This teaching from God's Word is designed to get you where you want to be—*on top!*

You can catch the *Believer's Voice of Victory* broadcast on your local, cable or satellite channels.

*Check your local listings for times and stations in your area.

Believer's Voice of Victory **Magazine**

Enjoy inspired teaching and encouragement from Kenneth and Gloria Copeland and guest ministers each month in the *Believer's Voice of Victory* magazine. Also included are real-life testimonies of God's miraculous power and divine intervention in the lives of people just like you!

It's more than just a magazine—it's a ministry.

To receive a FREE subscription to
Believer's Voice of Victory write to:

Kenneth Copeland Ministries
Fort Worth, Texas 76192-0001
Or call:
1-800-600-7395
(7 a.m.-5 p.m. CT)
Or visit our Web site at:
www.kcm.org

If you are writing from outside the U.S., please contact
the KCM office nearest you. Addresses for all Kenneth
Copeland Ministries offices are listed on the
previous page.